ON
SITE

The Construction
of a High-Rise

Text and photographs by
Richard Younker

ON SITE

Thomas Y. Crowell   New York

The comments by workers in the text
of *On Site* are not necessarily those
of the people shown in the photographs.

On Site: The Construction of a High-Rise
Copyright © 1980 by Richard Younker

All rights reserved. Printed in the United States
of America. No part of this book may be used
or reproduced in any manner whatsoever
without written permission except in the case
of brief quotations embodied in critical articles
and reviews. For information address Thomas
Y. Crowell, 10 East 53rd Street, New York, N.Y.
10022. Published simultaneously in Canada
by Fitzhenry & Whiteside Limited Toronto.

Designed by Al Cetta

Library of Congress Cataloging in Publication Data
Younker, Richard.
   On site, the construction of a high-rise.

    1. High-rise apartment buildings—Design
and construction. I. Title.
TH4820.Y68   1980   690'.8314
79-7889
ISBN 0-690-04003-2
ISBN 0-690-04004-0 lib. bdg.

1 2 3 4 5 6 7 8 9 10
First Edition

Acknowledgments

Special thanks to Angelo Polvere of the Mayfair Construction Company for encouragement and assistance, and for giving me unlimited access to Mayfair's Dearborn Park site at 820 South Federal; to Frank Santangelo and the Turner Construction Company for access to their sites at Three First National Plaza and 1100 Lake Shore Drive; to Crane Construction Company for access to their sites at Division and Wells and 2 North LaSalle; to Case International Corporation; to Soil Testing Service of Northbrook, Illinois; to Draper & Kramer, Inc., for access to their site at 33 West Monroe.

My gratitude to all the tradesmen, foremen, and superintendents who allowed me to photograph them, and who willingly shared their knowledge and experiences during lunch hours and coffee breaks.

Also, thanks to Joe Rowley of The Darkroom.

"Most of the public thinks a building just happens, it jumps up out of the ground. Well, nothing could be farther from the truth. It takes a lot of work, thousands and thousands of man-hours, maybe a million, to construct a building like this. You'd be surprised!"

—A carpentry foreman

Introduction

There are two basic types of modern high-rise building construction—steel frame and concrete frame. The main reason I chose concrete-frame construction as the subject of this book is that it often employs the flying-form system. Wood and steel forms, sometimes as large as thirty by fifty feet and ten feet high, are constructed at the building site and then lifted by crane to an upper level where they serve as temporary supports for the concrete floor poured over them. A few days later, they are eased out and "flown" again by crane to a higher level, the process being repeated until the building reaches its highest point and is "topped out."

In steel-frame construction, members are partially assembled at steel mills far from the building site, and upon arrival at the site are lifted and fitted into place. This phase of steel construction is done separately from the other phases, such as pouring concrete and installing plumbing. In concrete construction the various tradesmen work in unison, rarely more than a few hours apart. There is visibly more team-work, more human effort, and that's what interested me most about the industry—the people who form and raise and "fly" the buildings.

It takes anywhere from one and a half to three years to construct a high-rise concrete building, so I chose to photo-graph at six separate building sites where the work was in different stages. The buildings were not all the same size, and the sequence of events was not always the same, but the work was performed with very similar techniques and equipment. For in construction, when a successful method is discovered, it is quickly pressed into service by the major and smaller contractors, and remains in use until something better is conceived.

ON SITE

Above: Detaching a cylinder, which is driven into the earth to collect soil samples. *Right:* A field test is made to measure the soil's compactness.

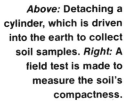

There are four major phases in the erection of a modern concrete high-rise building—excavation and laying the foundation; erecting the frame, or superstructure; enclosing the building; and finishing the interior.

The Foundation

Five feet below Chicago, the ground is made of clay. As you go deeper into the earth, the clay becomes increasingly hard, and at fifty-five feet it is almost like rock. This material is called hardpan, and structures of twenty stories or fewer may have their foundations on it. At eighty-five feet there is a layer of boulder till, or crumbled rock. To reach bedrock, or solid rock, where buildings of forty stories or more are anchored, you must dig over one hundred feet below the earth's surface. Interestingly, in New York City, bedrock is often less than ten feet underground.

Before a backhoe or front-end loader chews out its first shovelful of dirt, soil tests are made. Cylinders driven into the ground to various depths are retrieved with soil samples inside, and the samples are sent to laboratories for tests. What type of material—sand, clay, or rock—is below the site? How dense is the soil, and what is its water content? And how much water can be added to or taken out of the soil before it turns to mud or dust and "fails"? The answers to these questions tell a construction company what its costs for excavation will be.

3

The operator of a front-end loader during excavation.
Opposite: A front-end loader drops an iron weight onto large rocks to break them into smaller pieces.

The excavation itself takes place in several stages. First a backhoe scoops up shovelfuls of earth and pours them into dump trucks. Deeper down, it forages for small rocks, bricks, and wiring from the building previously on the site. And whenever the backhoe reaches obstacles, a front-end loader helps it out. For example, this machine takes in its teeth a great iron weight and drops it onto rocks too large for lifting, breaking them into "bite-sized" pieces. Or it batters down a basement wall uncovered by the backhoe. Or it simply digs and dumps along with the backhoe. After two months, when the hole is ten feet deep, the site supervisor says to a passerby, "Those two machines look lost out there, don't they? Well, come back in about two weeks and there'll be so much equipment, you'll hardly have a place to put your foot down!"

Indeed, the next phase—sinking of caissons—is a busy and crowded period. Much of a building's weight is supported by a series of shafts that are sunk fifty-five to one hundred and five feet underground and end at the structure's roof. Below the earth, the shaft is called a caisson. Above ground, it is referred to as a column.

5

A great auger, eight feet in circumference, is placed at the end of a crane. It bores the first caisson hole. After about five minutes' drilling, its ridges caked with mud, the auger is lifted and removed a distance from the hole. It rotates rapidly, throwing off hundred-pound chunks of wet, solid earth that could easily break your leg if you were hit.

Several more drillings and half an hour later, the hole reaches a depth of about thirty-six feet. (It used to take two

On the left a cylinder has been lowered into a caisson hole drilled by a giant auger. The auger, which is on the right, appears larger than actual size because of its closeness to the camera.

An ironworker ties together the reinforcing bars, or "rebars," of a caisson cage. The reel on his hip contains the tie wire.

shifts, working round the clock, half a day or more to reach that level.) A thirty-six-foot-long hollow metal cylinder, or "sleeve," is then lowered by crane into the hole. The sleeve will prevent a cave-in of the shaft wall and drifting of soil from underneath nearby buildings.

On another part of the site, two ironworkers are constructing great circular cages of reinforcing rods or bars. "How much you think them rebars [reinforcing bars] weigh? At thirteen pounds a foot and thirty foot apiece, that's four hundred pounds, and two of us to lift 'em. Here! Look at this; feel that muscle. You think that's hard? That's relaxed—I ain't tensin' up. That's soft as I can make it.

"I can make a lot of money in this racket. But that's 'cause I know everybody; I been in the business for twenty-five years. If I was to get laid off tomorrow, eight-thirty in the morning, I'd have another job by ten. But this ain't no picnic. You take those wire cutters and see what you can do with 'em. See that? And we gotta make hundreds of those [cuts] every day. Sometimes your thumb just closes on your fingers; they stay together till you go in the shack and warm 'em up.

"We work three hundred and sixty-five days a year. Rain, snow, everything. On days so cold no one would walk outdoors, we're out here fourteen, sixteen hours. All the other tradesmen go home, we stay."

Within two hours, bedrock is reached. But because of pressure from glaciers retreating across this part of the country ten thousand years ago, the upper crust of the bedrock is fractured. So a rock-coring bucket with teeth around its outer edge replaces the auger and chews several feet into the bedrock.

Next two men in raincoats with pails and shovels descend into the hole to clean up any rock debris that the bucket could not retrieve. They are followed by the soil-testing engineer, hired by the building owner, who determines at last that solid bedrock has been reached.

Now a sixty-five-foot-high cylinder or "casing," which replaces the sleeve, is lowered into the shaft and secured there. Concrete is poured almost continuously into it. Then another cylinder, or "corrugated shell," of about thirty feet is slipped over the casing. The caisson cage is lowered inside the shell and on top of the pour, and the final thirty feet of concrete is poured into it. The caisson is complete after a temporary cap is placed over it.

Meanwhile, the pile driver pounds in forty-foot "soldier beams" around the outer edge of the site. First a beam is maneuvered by crane into a tall upright frame, or "lead"; then a great weight, or pile driving head, is driven up and down upon the beam, perhaps a hundred times, sinking it within two to three noisy minutes. Later, boards are cut and fit between the beams, forming a temporary wall that will

Opposite: **A soldier beam is placed within the housing of a pile driver before being pounded into the ground. Note the soldier beams on the left which have already been sunk.**

8

prevent cave-ins of the site and the street beyond.

"I started out as a pile driver forty years ago. You know what kind a' noise dey make. After t'ree months I get a bad headache. So I go see this doctor in Hammond [Indiana], where I was working. He said, what you do for a living? I say, operate a pile driver. He say, I tell you how to cure them headaches. Find another job. So I get on as a carpenter for about t'ree months, but that give out so I go back to the pile driver. And dot's da way it's been. A little bit a' carpenter, a little bit a' pile driving, back and forth, back and forth.

"You seen that filtration plant at Navy Pier? You know how many piles they got to drive out there? A hundred fifty

t'ousand! Five pile drivers going at one time. What a racket they made, you don't believe it! Now my right ear's dead, don't hear nothin', and the left only a little when I turn the machine [hearing aid] up. Today they got these earplugs, but I never did like 'em."

This particular building is to have ninety-six caissons, forty-eight sunk into bedrock, forty-eight into hardpan. After they are completed, backhoes and a front-end loader dig out six more feet from the entire pit, exposing the caisson tops. Then the basement slab is poured, columns are formed over the caissons, the first-floor slab is poured, and the project reaches ground level.

A front-end loader during the second phase of excavation.

The Superstructure

Left: **Workers fill a grade beam with concrete and agitate it to insure that it is distributed evenly.**
Right: **A concrete bucket is steadied directly above a wall form.**

On either side of a four-foot-deep trough, or "grade beam," around the edge of the structure, thick plywood boards are placed on end about eighteen inches apart. Concrete trucks back up to the trough, and down their metal chutes cascade oozy flows of concrete. As the trough fills, the concrete is agitated with a vibrator, which spreads it evenly and distributes its aggregate, or gravel content. A good deal of the building's weight will rest upon the grade beam, a load shared with the columns and caissons.

12

Now the roar of engines is replaced by the competing sounds of handsaws and sledgehammers, the clink of metal scaffolds being piled one on top of another, and the jangle of rebars dropping over caisson tops—the slap of wooden forms against the rebars, and the nearly silent whir of the crane controls as workers on top of the forms grab at dangling concrete buckets. Then whoosh! Workers empty the contents of the buckets down the forms, over and over, until the forms are full and only three feet of rebar fingers remain uncovered. In thirty-six hours the concrete is firm and workers can strip away the wooden forms.

Left: **The concrete drops into the form.** *Right:* **A carpenter strips the form away from a concrete column while holding onto its protruding steel rebars.**

13

At this moment, when the ground floor is cluttered with columns in all stages of growth, the erection of the stationary crane begins. This machine will save tens of thousands of man-hours, and numerous backaches as well. Its purpose is to lift from ground to floor or from floor to floor a variety of items—buckets of concrete, rebars, plumbing stacks, electrical conduits, and bulky items like bathtubs and drywall.

First two long beams are crossed on the ground in the middle of the site. Next, a section of tower is lifted by a temporary crane and fitted on top of the beams. Support bars are bolted to the beams and braced against the tower. Sometimes the holes for connecting parts do not quite coincide, so a crowbar or sledgehammer is used to clang them into alignment.

Another section is set above the first, and four ironworkers climb up inside to bolt the two sections together. They wait on top of the second section for a third, which they guide and bolt into place, continuing this way until the tower is nearly ninety feet tall.

Two ironworkers bolt together the top section of the crane tower.

The ironworkers now secure a cabin above the tower, where the operator will sit. Out from the cabin they extend a sixty-foot crane boom, assembled in twenty-foot sections on the ground, and then they string out wires and the hook that will grasp and carry building materials. Finally, they ride up the company banner and fix it near the top of the tower, where it will always be visible.

In the shadow of the tower, work continues on the construction of the first level. Surveyors eye their instruments and help determine where scaffolding is to be placed. A

16

carpenter then sets up a scaffold while another carpenter places the next one ten feet behind it. A steady stream of laborers keep these supports stockpiled against nearby columns for ready use.

A more varied storage area is built up just south of the site. In this fifty-square-foot area there is material for immediate use—two-by-fours, four-by-fours, plywood, and rebars —as well as supplies that may not be used for weeks, but which can withstand weathering—scaffolding and plumbing pipes, stacks, and sleeves.

Top: An ironworker signals to the crane operator as the crane boom is assembled. *Bottom:* Carpenters erect the scaffolding that will hold the planks and boards for the second floor deck.

Building supplies, such as rebars, planks, and plumbing pipes, can be stored outdoors. At the upper right a high-rise is beginning to go up.

A group of carpenters measure, saw, and nail the beginning of a platform on top of the ground-floor outer columns.
Others place the second level of scaffolding, which will
reach to the top of the first floor. Long four-by-fours are
hand-lifted up and placed over the second level of scaffolds,
forming a wooden gridwork over the entire area.

Now the crane begins to earn its keep. It hauls up a dozen
boards and deposits them on the first-floor roof, or the se-
cond-floor "deck." The boards are nailed onto the lat-
ticework of four-by-fours. Within a day, the entire deck will

20

be boarded over, except for the protruding rebars and the crane area.

The crane lifts cages of pretied rebars, the supports or skeletons for columns. Ironworkers tie these cages to the exposed column stubs so that they, in turn, will stick up above the third-floor deck when the second floor is finished.

One hundred yards south of the structure, the flying forms are being assembled. These are the temporary wood and steel supports for the fourth through twenty-fifth floors. One of the workers assembling the forms talks about herself:

Top: **Carpenters secure plywood boards over the planks and scaffolding.** *Bottom:* **An ironworker secures a rebar cage, which will be the support for a column.**

21

Right: On the ground a carpenter nails planks together for the construction of flying forms. *Below:* A flying form is pushed out from under the ceiling it has supported for several days. The man on the far right is instructing the crane operator.

"The other women from my carpentry course are working on home construction. Mostly suburban houses and wood materials. I like concrete. That's what I started with and it's what I know best. You see, someday I want to be superintendent of a site. Not just frame houses. That would only be a token for a woman. I want to be superintendent at a high-rise like this one."

Once the concrete ceiling of the second floor—that is, the deck of the third—has been poured, the crane lifts a form to the deck, and laborers and carpenters help lower it to a certain spot. On the ground, a strong wire is looped around another form, the wire is attached to the hook of the crane, and the ungainly form is "flown" to its perch on the deck, next to the first. A carpenter nails a plywood board between them.

Forms are flown from the ground until the entire third-floor deck is covered. Plumbing and electrical work is done, steel reinforcing rods are laid out in a grid, and concrete for the columns and floor is poured. The next two decks are created in the same manner, but after that, forms will no longer be lifted from the ground. They will be flown from floor to floor until the building reaches its highest level and is "topped out."

Down on the third floor, where the first group of forms has been holding up the ceiling for nine days, a gang of four men appears. They turn jackscrews that lower the top of one of the flying forms seven or eight inches. The crane's hook is attached to a wire girdling the center of the form. Then, with a series of vigorous nudges from the men on the third floor, the form edges its way out into space. A little more, a little more, and it is airborne, twisting slightly, but then steadying for its lift up to the sixth-floor deck. All day this will continue,

A form eases out, about to "fly" by crane to the deck three stories higher.

until all the forms from the third floor are in place on the sixth floor.

Because the third-floor concrete is not entirely "cured," wooden four-by-fours are wedged between floor and ceiling, where they will remain for another two weeks. But now the building is ready to go up at a rather rapid pace. Three days from now, the forms on the fourth floor will be moved to the seventh floor; three days after that the ones on the fifth floor will be lifted to the eighth floor; and so forth on up to the twenty-fifth floor.

Top: **A flying form is guided onto the deck between two other forms.** *Bottom:* **A carpenter nails down one of the boards that joins two flying forms.**

25

By the time four forms have landed on any one floor, carpenters have appeared. Some of them calculate distances with tape measures and then snap red and blue chalk lines down with coated strings. Others consult plans or blueprints, and stoop to draw a circle or mark an X. All day long they follow the landing forms, marking plans on the deck sections.

The next morning, just twenty minutes after the mid-autumn sunrise, the deck is busy with workers. Momentarily they refer to blueprints, then look to the lines chalked the previous day. Soon electricians are grouping and tying together fistfuls of conduits, snaking them across the deck toward a terminal that another electrician is securing. Nearby, a carpenter drills a series of holes through the deck. Down them plumbers drop pipes that connect to pipes on the floor below. (In other types of construction, plumbing pipes are "flagpoled," or shoved upward through the ceiling to the deck above.) Next the "sleeves," or receptacles, are placed over the pipes and temporarily capped so foreign matter—particularly concrete, which will smother the deck tomorrow—won't fall inside.

"Landing iron"

Ironworkers appear and further crowd the working space. They start placing thin wire supports, two inches high and three feet long, on which the first layer of rebars will rest. One support goes over a conduit, another beside the protruding top of a rebar cage, and a third beside a stack.

An electrician complains, "They're always getting in the way."

The ironworker replies, "Without us, the buildin' wouldn't stand up." Then he walks to the edge of the deck, and, with

28

a series of hand motions, signals the crane operator to lift a ton of rebars from the ground to an uncluttered spot. "That's what we call 'landin' iron,'" he says.

The ironworker continues. "Now, after lunch, when all these fellows get out of our way [they will be doing electrical and plumbing work on the other side], we're going to lay out a grid of these rebars across this half of the roof, like John's startin' to do over there. These are what strengthen the concrete. And now look at this—you see how these horizontal rebars extend into where we're going to tie the vertical rebar cage tomorrow? That transfers the concrete's weight to the column so that the floor doesn't entirely support itself. The column helps out. And later this afternoon, we're going to put a second layer of rebars on supports called 'high chairs' about eight inches on top of the first."

Left: **An ironworker with his hands full of "high chairs," or the supports for rebars.** *Right:* **He ties the second layer of rebars to the "high chair" supports.**

29

Left: Concrete pours from the truck into a waiting bucket. *Right:* A laborer pulls a lever on the bucket to release the concrete.

The following morning begins well. At 8:00 A.M. two concrete trucks rumble up to the building site. Chutes are attached to their back ends while a mixture of cement, water, sand, and stone aggregate sloshes around inside. Five minutes later, a load of concrete is poured into a waiting bucket. A hand signal from the ground is repeated by another on the edge of the deck, and the crane operator pushes a small lever. The metal bucket lurches skyward, four tons—two cubic yards—of concrete in its well.

"Concrete is such a fascinating material," the superintendent says. "Just think of the transformation it undergoes— from this gooey, pliant mass that you can work into any shape you want, into something hard enough to walk on, within half an hour. As a matter of fact, with a variety of

30

finishing tools we can make concrete so slick that if there was to be a little rain over it, it would be every bit as treacherous as an ice surface. That's why we have to rough it over with a spiked broom in order to have it pass the building codes."

Responding to additional hand signals, the crane operator maneuvers the bucket so that it hovers just three feet above the deck. There, a cement mason, balancing on the springy rebars, steadies the load, resteadies it, and suddenly pulls a lever. Splash! Part of the bucket's load cascades down, running over the thick iron rebars, burying plumbing stack bases, conduits, and the two thin layers of rebars—in short, covering everything secured the previous day.

31

The strike-off is used to level the concrete. It must be lifted over obstacles like plumbing pipes and rebars.

Now the hurry-up work begins. Cement laborers wade into the mixture. (In home construction they are aptly called "puddlers.") Two of them, using the backs of their shovels, roughly level the pour, while a third dips a vibrator into the concrete to spread it evenly around the rebars and plumbing stacks.

They are followed immediately by laborers whose tool is called a "strike-off." This ten-foot-long two-by-four with high handles is pushed forward and sideways, in almost one

motion, to refine the leveling the previous workers have done.

Next come the cement masons. Their "bull float" has a twelve-foot handle and a thin two-foot magnesium blade. Very gently they sweep it across the concrete, to help push aggregate down from the top, and withdraw it, coaxing water up from the bottom of the mix. Back and forth, back and forth they sweep, to the metal clanging of the ironworkers gridding the other side of the deck.

The long-handled bull float is used to smooth a fresh pour. The man bending over is doing rough leveling with a small strike-off.

33

This cement mason gives a final smoothing to the concrete with hand trowels. Behind him is a machine trowel, which he pushes like a lawn mower to level tiny ridges left by the bull floats.

Soon the concrete is hard enough to walk on, but not perfectly smooth. A series of low ridges breaks its surface. The finisher starts his machine trowel. As he pushes it, its rotating blade levels the tops of the ridges. He stops and adjusts the blade so that it will cut more. Finally, on hands and knees, he sweeps hand trowels across the deck, to sand it to a smooth, even finish.

Now ironworkers tie steel rebar cages, constructed on the ground the day before, to the rebars protruding from the columns of the floor below. By late afternoon half of these will have forms placed over them, and concrete will have been poured down the forms.

Building codes require that the concrete on each floor be tested for hardness. Twenty-inch-high cylinders are filled with concrete from a pour off each deck. At a laboratory, the concrete is placed in a machine that acts like a vise. Pressure is applied, and when the minutest crack appears, the number of pounds of pressure the material can withstand is determined. Tests are conducted after one day of setting, or hardening, after one week, two weeks, and four weeks.

On-site inspection occurs as well. Once a week, the architect—whose responsibilities go far beyond drawing up the building plans—makes a tour of the building. Is the concrete being poured properly? Is it being vibrated too vigorously or not vigorously enough? Are the rebars tied securely? These are some of the things he must check.

Although he is watchful, the architect maintains a good deal of respect for the workers on the deck. "I don't know how they do it when they're putting down the embedded items [conduits, rebars, and so forth]; they hardly ever have to look at the plans. They just seem to know where everything goes. And it has to be exact! Oh, I know they've been doing it a long time and all, but it still amazes me."

As the building rises, other events occur on the lower floors. For example, a temporary elevator is constructed on the north exterior of the building to carry up workers and heavy materials.

A site superintendent

Left: Carpenters build a form for a concrete stairway. *Right:* A laborer vibrates the concrete to spread it evenly around the rebars in the stair frames.

When the building is ten stories high, construction on the stairs begins. The stairs will also help the movement of laborers, and of light materials, between floors. First two wooden forms are set between floors. Rebars are placed over them, and riser forms, which give the stairs their shape, are nailed to the rebars. The next morning—"or whenever there's concrete left from pouring the deck; we're second-class citizens," jokes one of the carpenters building the stairs—concrete is poured.

From about the fourth floor up, concrete for the stairs is brought by the elevator in wheelbarrows. On lower floors, concrete is pumped directly from the truck it is mixed in, and is called "pumpcrete." (Concrete sprayed or shot onto structures is called "shotcrete.")

The stair pour is shoveled, vibrated, leveled, and troweled

36

smooth. And a day later, the support frames and riser forms are removed and replaced with two-by-four temporary wedges that hold up the stairs as they finish setting.

Interestingly, similar structures built by the same company almost never progress in the same way. Good "stair men" may not be available until the twentieth deck has been poured. Elevator rails might be set any time between the pouring of the tenth and twenty-fifth decks. Concrete, too, may be unavailable, and the entire construction site may be quiet for a week or more. If concrete is scarce, the workday may be lengthened by several hours. "We didn't get finished pouring the deck until after nine o'clock last night. Concrete just kept dribbling in, dribbling in, a little bit at a time. Matter of fact, we didn't get any the first three hours after lunch."

We have already seen how smooth the concrete is made

Left: An elevator constructor drops a plumb line to set an elevator car. *Right:* Concrete for lower floors is pumped directly from the truck. For higher floors, it is lifted by crane.

37

Left: **A cement mason uses a "giraffe" to sand down ridges on the ceilings.** *Right:* **Another cement mason spreads a patching compound over small holes.**

on each deck. But what about the undersides of the decks, the ceilings? Though they are level, because concrete is poured onto flat forms, they have two flaws.

Ridges of concrete, created by seams where forms were joined, are corrected by a "giraffe." A cement mason walks this machine, pushing a coarse, rapidly rotating disc at the end of a long neck against the ceiling. The "giraffe" makes a lot of noise, creates a lot of dust, but it smooths the ceiling in very little time.

Depressions in the ceiling caused by flaws in the wood of the forms are dispatched with equal ease. Another mason loads the blade of a long-handled spatula with a patching compound and strokes it across those areas.

A floor above the cement masons are the safety workers. According to building safety codes, they stretch taut, thick wires from column to column, fencing in the open spaces.

The job of sheet-metal workers, nicknamed "tin knockers," is to install the cooling system. They measure, shape, hammer, and bend sleeves and ducts, which go from the basement to an upper-floor cooling plant and back down again. One floor at a time they "tilt" the finished shafts upward through openings and set them in place.

Above: Safety codes require that protective wire cables be installed around each floor. *Right:* Sheet-metal workers install metal ducts for air conditioning.

A plumber coats a pipe joint with a compound for a tight seal.

Several weeks later, plumbers, kneeling and squatting like baseball catchers, shift across the floor. They coat slender, silver-colored hot- and cold-water pipes with a compound for a tight seal. Then they thread them into other pipes and fit them in among the larger, dark iron waste pipes, twisting, tapping, wrenching, and measuring until the pipes fit snugly.

"You see that rubber disc up at the ceiling where the pipe goes through?" asks one of the plumbers. "You know what that's for? Well, see, in the morning everybody's takin' showers, shavin' and everything; they're using a lot of hot water. That means the pipe's gonna expand. So we give it a little space between the pipe and the ceiling. The disc can take it up. Same thing later on when the hot water goes off and the pipe starts to cool a little bit. Then the pipe contracts, right? The disc takes that in too."

A week later, more plumbers. They set bathtubs down against pipes in areas swept clean of dust, cement, and

40

metal scraps. They align and connect them, making sure they're level, and secure them to the floor.

While work is being done in the roofed-over areas, lit by occasional bare bulbs, the building progresses at deck level. A floor every three days, up and up, with few breaks in scheduling. At penthouse level the building cooling plant is installed. And one week later, on a sunny afternoon with only two or three patchy clouds in the sky, the climbing stops. The final floor has been reached. By three-thirty the last bucket of concrete is poured and everyone lets out a yell.

"We used to have big parties when we topped out a building," remarks one of the men, "but not anymore. It's just ho-hum, and on to the next one tomorrow."

The foreman walks to the edge of the building and waves to someone, probably the superintendent, twenty-five stories below. He returns.

"Bein' up here doesn't bother me," he says. "What makes it easy is if you work your way up. When you're on the first floor you look over the side, and that's nothin'. The second floor isn't bad either. And so forth. I was on a building at Lake Shore Drive and Foster. We got up to the fortieth floor and I looked down to the ground one day and shouted, I don't know, something like, hey, we need some iron—or maybe it was stacks—up here! Of course there was no way he could hear me. He couldn't a' heard me with a bullhorn with the wind blowin' and everything. But you get so used to it, goin' up floor by floor, that when you get near the top, it's like stoppin' at the edge of the curb. Like you're shakin' hands with the earth."

Enclosing the Building

Because it employs so many workers at relatively high wages, a construction company has to maneuver efficiently. Thus, on a day when forms are being flown up to the twelfth deck, seven cement masons and laborers are called to the ground, where the lobby is to be poured. Or on another day, when concrete is not available, they may leave for a site halfway across the city where their skills can be put to use.

One morning, when the skeleton of the building is only 60 percent complete, a new group of laborers appears on the site. Unloading planks and hoists, plywood, chain wire, and winches, they begin the first step in bricking up the building: building a scaffold. Something like a high-rise window washer's scaffold, in that it supports workers and materials and can be winched upward from floor to floor, this scaffold reaches around the entire building and can hold the weight of half a dozen bricklayers, along with tons of bricks and mortar. It may have a sturdy wooden overhang to protect the bricklayers from objects that might fall accidentally from floors above.

Opposite: **Workers level fresh concrete in the lobby of the building.** *Above:* **A shelf angle is installed to support bricks.** *Right:* **A scaffold supports the bricklayers.**

In the recently poured lobby, a man operates a circular, diamond-bladed saw, cutting bricks in half and angling off sections to be fitted on bay window corners. And for the previous month ironworkers have been screwing metal supports into the sides of the building to hold the actual brickwork. These supports, called "shelf angles," are fifteen feet long and are located at each floor level.

Bricklaying begins slowly, as do so many other operations. In this instance, pouring the lobby and moving materials delay progress. But once the bricklayers are above the first-floor level, the operation speeds up considerably. One worker alternately shovels sand and pours water and powder into a mortar mixing machine. The material is sloshed around until it forms a pastelike compound. It is then transferred to wheelbarrows, and other workers take it to the second floor and deposit it in generous shovelfuls along a row of working bricklayers.

Next it's over to piles of unopened brick. Workers break the steel bands wrapped around the bricks, load up a dolly, and move them to within easy reach of the bricklayers. A last, quick run past, prodding and overturning mortar with

Left: A diamond-bladed saw cuts bricks in half. *Right:* A bricklayer at work.

Installing window frames

shovel blades to keep it from stiffening, and it's back down in the elevator.

Attended to this way, the bricklayers work without interruption, joshing one another from behind trowel or level. First they lay a wall of concrete block, each bulky and gray, with three air chambers. Two inches in front of that they place the "house brick," or the "facing" wall. The resulting air pocket between the two walls insulates the building. After daubing mortar on either side and on top of a set brick, a bricklayer carefully places another over it and gently taps it with the handle of his trowel until it looks even. This process is repeated down the entire row. Then a level is used to check the bricks for evenness. If any brick is slightly raised, it is tapped farther into the fresh mortar.

Look at any brick wall; you will notice that the bricks are not piled directly on top of one another. Instead, one brick might cover half of each of the two below it. There are many different patterns of bricking, called "bonds" or "weaves," designed to give maximum strength. Their major difference, however, is in outward appearance; they are primarily artistic arrangements from which the architect may choose.

When all the bricklaying, rough plumbing, and stair setting is completed to about the twelfth-floor level, windows are installed. Frames are set in place and secured, glass is lifted and placed inside the frames, and a sealer is applied.

The Interior

"Paul, do we have any problems with high-rise number four at our downtown project?"

"Well, Bob, I know it's a long way down the road, but what are we going to do about the roof? Shouldn't we start thinking about renting equipment to siphon water off and pipe it to the ground? Maybe hooking up with the sewer?"

"I think you're talking about a lot of money there. Do we have it in our budget?"

"Well—but don't you think we should do it?"

"Paul, I think we'll have the roof poured soon enough, so that by the time we start to get a lot of winter moisture, the concrete will be perfectly solid."

"You want to let the roof pond [let moisture form on its surface], then?"

"Yes, I think we can do that." And, speaking into a tape recorder: *"In answer to Paul's question about moisture on the roof at high-rise number four, we will let the roof pond."*

In a biweekly meeting attended by city officials and various foremen, this construction executive and an architect are referring to one of the conditions that "closes in" a building—that is, completing the roof. Bricking up the walls and putting in the windows are the other two. Then materials like drywall, which can be damaged by weather, can be stored safely in the building until they are installed.

When a building is closed in, construction sounds no longer blend with the ones outside—with truck horns and squealing tires. Instead they grow louder and remain longer, rocketing from wall to wall. There are the sharp reports of large staple guns as workers attach metal braces, called "tracks," along floors and ceilings; the muffled buzzes of electric drills screwing studs at right angles to these tracks; and the sound of drywall being drilled to their supports.

After the drywall ceilings and walls are up, a gooey plasterlike compound is placed over the seams. A tape about four inches wide is placed over that, followed by another layer of the compound. Later the seams are sanded until they are smooth and ready for painting.

Left: **Attaching drywall.** *Below:* **A worker applies a compound to the seams in the ceiling drywall. Taped seams of wall sections can be seen in the background.**

Once the walls are up, most of the other interior operations fall into place. In a bathroom, a ceramic tile man dabs mastic on the three walls above the tub. First seated, then standing, he draws tiles from a stack and places them against the wall. Soon he has covered everything except the corners, with room on either side for a little less than half a tile the whole way up and down. He carefully measures the distance, adjusts a cutting machine on the floor, and slices the tiles to size. And, for the most part (occasionally one must be nudged a bit), they all fit easily into place.

"You know what I like about this job?" says the tiler as he grabs his gear and hurries to the next room. "It's the variety. We're at a different place almost every week. Outdoors a lot too. I do terraces, patios, even put in the tiles for swimming pools. And sometimes, for lobbies, each one of the tiles might be part of a mosaic, so I've got to piece it together. And you're always trying to cut and fit in an extra piece, just like a puzzle. Oh, it's always interesting."

48

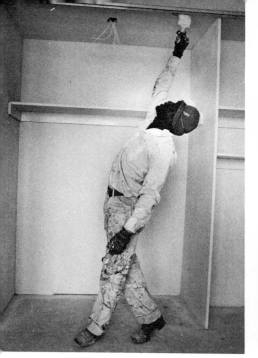

The plumber who follows the tiler a day later installs toilets. First he pries up and removes a cap that has temporarily sealed the drainpipe. Next, the bowl is flipped upside down, gummed around its bottom, turned upright, and aligned with the drain. It is then attached to the floor. The toilet back is set in place, its evenness tested with a level, and, after a few test flushes, the top is fitted.

The "finish carpenters" are next. Some place preassembled cabinets in bathrooms or kitchens. Others install sliding doors in front of wall-length closets in the living rooms. Still another carpenter, having spent two days screwing hinges onto doors, is ready to "hang," or put them in place. He carries a door on his back to the door frame before each apartment. He then backs the door up to a two-inch-high ramp that helps him guide the hinges onto the wall bolts, and secures the door. If it doesn't fit exactly, he wedges it up or down until positioning is perfect.

Workmen unwrap faucets and screw them into sink bowls

Left: A painter puts the finishing touches on a closet interior. *Right:* A carpenter stands in front of a door he has just hung. He spent the previous day screwing hinges onto doors.

49

and line the bowls up in the hallways for the plumbers.

Coiled heating elements, which attach to the conduits embedded in concrete, are placed around the baseboards, and sheet-metal covers are placed over them.

Prospective tenants inspect model apartments on the first floor. The painters seem to quicken their strokes now, coating walls with an off-white and rolling a light tan over balconies. Wooden floors go down in strips. And all of a sudden, the number of laborers decreases. You notice one day there are no more drywallers or plumbers, fewer carpenters. There goes the "door man," with his bulky satchel in hand, and he will not be back again. Construction noises subside too.

For that matter, there is no more poring over of blueprints as foreman and laborer try to tell, between wind and snow, the right placement of a pipe or conduit. Long gone is the stationary crane that towered above the deck, and the iron it landed.

Just a few finishing touches now. The elevator car is installed and regulated, its controls set so it will stop level with each floor. Ranges and refrigerators are taken up by freight elevator and wheeled to their assigned quarters. "It's starting to look like a building now!"

But before a lost crowbar, saw, or level is retrieved and carried home; before the last clod of tracked-in clay or crushed coffee cup is swept up; before it is forgotten that so many people have stooped, hauled, hollered, carried, sweated, balanced, hammered, and sawed; before all this, one afternoon, after everyone has gone home, if you walk about the echoing hallways or step onto the windswept roof, and if you cock your ear and hold your breath, you can still hear the voices . . .

"Item: So in response to Paul's question, we won't build any temporary drainage apparatus; we'll just let the roof pond."

"Say, son, grab you a heater."
"What's a heater?"
"A heater's a shovel. 'Cause if you use it, it's gonna keep you warm."

"One time we did a job, we put up a hospital near Tangier. Right on the Mediterranean. Oh, that was beautiful! You had those yellow dunes, those sand fingers that would stretch right into the ocean that was so blue you couldn't believe it! And then the sun would come up like a great big orange ball. Wow! We were on that job for two years, and it was like every morning you'd go to work to see some beautiful Technicolor movie. I swear!"

"On days so cold no one would walk outdoors, we're out here fourteen, sixteen hours. All the other tradesmen go home, we stay."

"Most of the public thinks a building just happens, it jumps up out of the ground. Well, nothing could be farther from the truth. It takes a lot of work, thousands and thousands of man-hours, maybe a million, to construct a building like this. You'd be surprised!"

For Richard Younker, *On Site* was a chance to pursue his three favorite activities: writing, taking pictures, and talking to people. His photo essays, which have appeared frequently in Chicago Sunday magazines, reflect his affection for the people of that city and his interest in their lives and work.

In the past Mr. Younker has been a mailman, sixth grade teacher, encyclopedia salesman, billing clerk, public aid worker, employment counselor, actor, and singer. Within the past few years, his poetry and photographs have appeared in various national magazines. *On Site* is his first book.